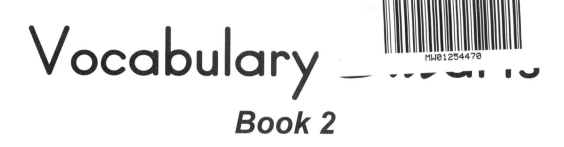

Vocabulary Smarts

Book 2

Series Titles:
Vocabulary Smarts Book 1
Vocabulary Smarts Book 2
Vocabulary Smarts Book 3

Written by
Judy Wilson Goddard

Graphics by
Brad Gates
Anna Chaffin

Edited by
Patricia Gray

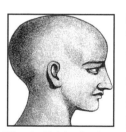

© 2008
THE CRITICAL THINKING CO.™
Phone: 800-458-4849 Fax: 831-393-3277
www.CriticalThinking.com
P.O. Box 1610 • Seaside • CA 93955-1610
ISBN 978-1-60144-173-7

Printed in the United States of America

Introduction

The vocabulary words taught in this book are the words that students encounter most frequently in school settings (first 1000 word lists). To give students a deeper understanding of these words and improve thinking and writing skills, students are asked to classify word pairs and then use at least two of the words in a sentence. Simple definitions are given to help students identify meaning and learn dictionary skills.

The book is divided into halves. The first half covers four skills (past/present verbs, singular/plural nouns, antonyms, and synonyms). The second half covers four additional skills (contractions, compound words, homophones, and pronouns).

About The Author

JUDY WILSON GODDARD has worn many hats; she served as a teacher and administrator in both private and public school settings, working with pre-school through college level students. Throughout her diverse career, she always maintained that critical thinking was important for all levels. Since her retirement, she has continued to promote critical thinking skills by writing books for children. She is the author of many books that apply critical thinking skills to a wide range of academic disciplines. She holds three degrees in education from Georgia State University: Bachelors, Masters, and Specialist.

This book is dedicated to my daughters, Joy and Janet, who are critical thinkers, and to my six grandchildren, with hope that they too will be critical thinkers and that their apples won't always have to be red!

TABLE OF CONTENTS

SECTION 1
Classifications Defined

Past tense and **present tense verbs** are words that tell the time something happened.

Past Tense		**Present Tense**
Yesterday <u>was</u> a good day.	⟶	Today <u>is</u> a good day.
Mom <u>cleaned</u> the house last Monday.	⟶	Mom <u>cleans</u> the house on Mondays.

Singular and **plural nouns** are words that refer to one (singular) or to more than one (plural).

Singular		**Plural**
dog	⟶	dogs
baby	⟶	babies
dish	⟶	dishes

Antonyms are words that have opposite meanings from one another.

big	⟶	little
hot	⟶	cold
light	⟶	dark

Synonyms are words with similar or identical meanings.

big	⟶	large
sea	⟶	ocean
laughs	⟶	giggles

SECTION 1

Circle the two words in each group that share a relationship
shown in the choice box. Write the letter of the relationship.
Then write a sentence using at least two of the words.

Choice Box

A. past tense/present tense verbs	B. singular/plural nouns
C. antonyms	D. synonyms

(accept)   (refuse)   film   farmer

___C___ relationship

I refuse to accept the film.

_____

_____

bob   cry   beautify   cried

_____ relationship

_____

_____

blind   uniform   blinds   united

_____ relationship

_____

_____

angry   favor   mad   favorite

_____ relationship

_____

_____

glue   fashion   paste   fasten

_____ relationship

_____

_____

Definitions

accept: to agree or consent to

angry: feeling or showing anger

beautify: to make or become beautiful

blind: a window covering having horizontal or vertical slats

blinds: window coverings

bob: to move quickly down and up

cried: wept

cry: to weep; shed tears

farmer: a person who farms

fashion: a style of dress

fasten: to attach firmly or securely in place

favor: something done or granted out of goodwill

favorite: a person or thing regarded with special favor

film: a thin layer or coating

glue: any of various solutions used as an adhesive

mad: angry

paste: a mixture used for causing paper or other material to stick to something

refuse: to decline to accept something offered

uniform: a standard type of clothing used for a job or school

united: to form a single whole unit

Circle the two words in each group that share a relationship shown in the choice box. Write the letter of the relationship. Then write a sentence using at least two of the words.

Choice Box

| A. past tense/present tense verbs | B. singular/plural nouns |
| C. antonyms | D. synonyms |

bodies   bend   boil   bent

_____ relationship

_____

_____

apart   fat   together   fault

_____ relationship

_____

_____

arise   banker   arose   bar

_____ relationship

_____

_____

agree   gain   dwelt   loss

_____ relationship

_____

_____

ash   farming   ashes   farther

_____ relationship

_____

_____

Definitions

agree: to have the same views
apart: separate
arise: to get up from sitting, lying, or kneeling
arose: got up from sitting, lying, or kneeling
ash: the powdery residue of matter that remains after burning
ashes: the powdery residues of matter that remains after burning
banker: a person employed by a bank, especially as an executive
bar: a piece of some solid substance, used as a guard or obstruction
bend: to force an object, from a straight form into a curved or angular one

bent: forced an object from a straight form into a curved or angular one
bodies: the physical structures of an animal or plant
boil: to change from a liquid to a gaseous state
dwelt: resides
farming: the business of operating a farm
farther: a long way off
fat: having too much flabby tissue
fault: a defect
gain: to get something desired
loss: failure to keep
together: as a group

Circle the two words in each group that share a relationship shown in the choice box. Write the letter of the relationship. Then write a sentence using at least two of the words.

Choice Box

A. past tense/present tense verbs	B. singular/plural nouns
C. antonyms	D. synonyms

asleep   bang   awake   banjo

_____ relationship

_____

_____

ate   barber   bare   eat

_____ relationship

_____

_____

bark   afar   barn   nearby

_____ relationship

_____

_____

awful   barefoot   terrible   barely

_____ relationship

_____

_____

beard   devil   beneath   angel

_____ relationship

_____

_____

Definitions

afar: from a distance
angel: a spiritual being
asleep: in a state of sleep
ate: chewed and swallowed food
awake: to wake up
awful: extremely bad
bang: a loud, sudden, explosive noise
banjo: a musical instrument of the guitar family
barber: a person whose occupation is to cut hair
bare: without covering or clothing
barefoot: without covering on the feet
barely: no more than

bark: the abrupt, harsh, explosive cry of a dog
barn: a building for storing hay, grain
beard: the growth of hair on the face of an adult man
beneath: below
devil: the supreme spirit of evil
eat: take food into the mouth and swallow for nourishment
nearby: close at hand
terrible: extremely bad

Circle the two words in each group that share a relationship shown in the choice box. Write the letter of the relationship. Then write a sentence using at least two of the words.

Choice Box

A. past tense/present tense verbs	B. singular/plural nouns
C. antonyms	D. synonyms

beg   dip   begged   dirt

_____ relationship

_____

_____

beginning   barrel   ending   basement

_____ relationship

_____

_____

berries   dirty   berry   decide

_____ relationship

_____

_____

borrow   unkind   lend   discover

_____ relationship

_____

_____

carpet   weary   rug   mitten

_____ relationship

_____

_____

Definitions

barrel: tub

basement: the underground story of a building

beg: to plead

begged: requested

beginning: the start

berries: any small, juicy fruits

berry: any small, juicy fruit like a strawberry

borrow: to take with the promise to return the same thing

carpet: a heavy fabric for covering floors

decide: to agree

dip: to dunk

dirt: any foul or filthy substance

dirty: soiled with dirt

discover: to gain knowledge of something previously unseen or unknown

ending: coming to an end

lend: to grant the use of something on condition that it will be returned

mitten: a hand covering enclosing the four fingers together and the thumb separately

rug: a thick fabric for covering part of a floor

unkind: inconsiderate

weary: physically or mentally exhausted by hard work

Circle the two words in each group that share a relationship shown in the choice box. Write the letter of the relationship. Then write a sentence using at least two of the words.

Choice Box

A. past tense/present tense verbs   B. singular/plural nouns

C. antonyms   D. synonyms

unless   coward   unknown   brave

_____ relationship

_____

_____

canary   uptown   wealth   bird

_____ relationship

_____

_____

brightness   upward   darkness   Mrs.

_____ relationship

_____

_____

cap   weave   orange   wove

_____ relationship

_____

_____

chocolate   misty   cocoa   mitt

_____ relationship

_____

_____

Definitions

bird: a feathered animal that flies
brave: possessing courage
brightness: lightness
canary: a bird that is often kept as a pet
cap: hat
chocolate: a candy
cocoa: powder made from seeds of the cacao
coward: a person who lacks courage in the face of danger
darkness: the state of being without light
misty: foggy
mitt: a rounded glove used in playing baseball
Mrs.: a title of respect used before the name of a married woman
orange: edible citrus fruit

unknown: unfamiliar
unless: except
uptown: to the upper part of a town or city
upward: toward a higher place
wealth: a great quantity of riches
weave: to interlace threads or yarns to form a fabric
wove: interlaced threads or yarns, forming a fabric

Circle the two words in each group that share a relationship shown in the choice box. Write the letter of the relationship. Then write a sentence using at least two of the words.

Choice Box

A. past tense/present tense verbs	B. singular/plural nouns
C. antonyms	D. synonyms

chose   whisper   whistle   choose

_____ relationship

_____

_____

cooked   web   raw   bakery

_____ relationship

_____

_____

cookie   wheel   cookies   whirl

_____ relationship

_____

_____

cooler   hotter   becoming   bee

_____ relationship

_____

_____

couch   beef   sofa   candle

_____ relationship

_____

_____

Definitions

bakery: a place where baked goods are made
becoming: grow to be
bee: an insect such as a bumblebee or honeybee
beef: the flesh of a cow
candle: a piece of wax with a wick
choose: to select from a number of possibilities
chose: selected from a number of possibilities
cooked: prepared food for eating by applying heat
cookie: a small flat cake made from sweetened dough
cookies: more than one cookie
cooler: moderately cold

couch: a piece of furniture for seating more than one person
hotter: having or giving off heat
raw: uncooked
sofa: couch
web: thin material spun by spiders
wheel: a circular frame arranged to revolve on an axis
whirl: to spin rapidly
whisper: to speak with soft, hushed sounds
whistle: to make a clear musical sound, or a high-pitched, warbling sound by the forcible expulsion of the breath

Circle the two words in each group that share a relationship shown in the choice box. Write the letter of the relationship. Then write a sentence using at least two of the words.

Choice Box

A. past tense/present tense verbs	B. singular/plural nouns
C. antonyms	D. synonyms

creep   beet   beggar   crept

_____ relationship

_____

_____

same   boast   alike   beauty

_____ relationship

_____

_____

dig   bin   dug   bet

_____ relationship

_____

_____

damp   wet   beast   beating

_____ relationship

_____

_____

divide   bead   multiply   beam

_____ relationship

_____

_____

Definitions

alike: having similar characteristics
bead: a small, usually round object with a hole through it, often strung with others of its kind in necklaces
beam: a light
beast: monster
beating: striking violently
beauty: attractiveness
beet: an plant that has a red root that is eaten
beggar: a person who begs
bet: to gamble
bin: a box for storage
boast: to speak with exaggeration, especially about oneself

creep: to move slowly with the body close to the ground
crept: moved slowly with the body close to the ground
damp: slightly wet
dig: to break up, turn over, or remove earth
divide: to separate into parts
dug: broke up, turned over, or removed earth
same: identical
multiply: to make many
wet: soaked with liquid

Circle the two words in each group that share a relationship shown in the choice box. Write the letter of the relationship. Then write a sentence using at least two of the words.

Choice Box

A. past tense/present tense verbs	B. singular/plural nouns
C. antonyms	D. synonyms

dawn   belt   bench   daybreak

_____ relationship

_____

_____

drive   welcome   drove   whale

_____ relationship

_____

_____

defend   beside   protect   bean

_____ relationship

_____

_____

die   bind   died   bib

_____ relationship

_____

_____

cute   begun   behave   pretty

_____ relationship

_____

_____

Definitions

bean: the edible seed of plants
begun: started
behave: to act in a particular way
belt: a band of flexible material for encircling the waist
bench: a long seat for several persons
beside: near
bib: a piece of cloth, plastic, or paper often tied under the chin of a child to protect the clothing while the child is eating
bind: to fasten or secure with a band
cute: attractive
dawn: the first appearance of daylight in the morning
daybreak: dawn
defend: to ward off attack from; guard against assault or injury
die: to cease to live; expire; become dead

died: to cease living
drive: to cause and guide the movement of a vehicle, an animal, etc.
drove: to have caused and guided the movement of a vehicle, an animal, etc.
pretty: good-looking
protect: to defend or guard from attack, invasion, loss, annoyance, insult, etc.
welcome: a word of kindly greeting, as to one whose arrival gives pleasure
whale: any of the larger marine mammals, having a fishlike body, forelimbs modified into flippers, and a head that is horizontally flattened

Circle the two words in each group that share a relationship shown in the choice box. Write the letter of the relationship. Then write a sentence using at least two of the words.

Choice Box

A. past tense/present tense verbs	B. singular/plural nouns
C. antonyms	D. synonyms

dive   birth   biscuit   dove

_____ relationship

_____

_____

double   bid   bigger   twin

_____ relationship

_____

_____

drank   bible   drink   bicycle

_____ relationship

_____

_____

dwarf   pane   giant   weed

_____ relationship

_____

_____

draw   Wednesday   heat   drew

_____ relationship

_____

_____

Definitions

bible: the collection of sacred writings of the Christian religion
bicycle: a vehicle with two wheels, pedals, handlebars, and a seat
bid: to express a greeting
bigger: larger
birth: an act of being born
biscuit: a kind of bread in small, soft cakes
dive: to plunge into water, especially headfirst
double: composed of two like parts
dove: plunged into water
drank: took liquid into the mouth and swallowed it
draw: to sketch someone or something in lines
drew: sketched someone or something in lines

drink: to take liquid into the mouth and swallow it
dwarf: a person of abnormally small stature
giant: a person or thing of unusually great size
heat: warmth
pane: a sheet of glass
twin: either of two persons or things closely resembling each other
Wednesday: the fourth day of the week, following Tuesday
weed: a valueless plant growing wild

Circle the two words in each group that share a relationship shown in the choice box. Write the letter of the relationship. Then write a sentence using at least two of the words.

Choice Box

A. past tense/present tense verbs	B. singular/plural nouns
C. antonyms	D. synonyms

empty   full   weigh   weep

_____ relationship

_____

_____

evil   blush   wicked   biting

_____ relationship

_____

_____

enter   blot   exit   bite

_____ relationship

_____

_____

fake   baseball   false   bitter

_____ relationship

_____

_____

fed   blackness   feed   blanket

_____ relationship

_____

_____

Definitions

baseball: a game of ball between two nine-player teams usually played for nine innings on a field

bite: to tear with the teeth

biting : cutting with the teeth

bitter: sour

blackness: darkness

blanket: a large piece of soft fabric used especially for warmth as a bed covering

blot: a spot or stain

blush: to redden, as from embarrassment

empty: containing nothing

enter: to come or go into

evil: morally wrong or bad

exit: a way or passage out

fake: phony

false: wrong

fed: gave food to

feed: to give food to

full: completely filled

weep: to express grief, sorrow, or emotion by shedding tears

weigh: to measure according to weight

wicked: evil or morally bad

Circle the two words in each group that share a relationship shown in the choice box. Write the letter of the relationship. Then write a sentence using at least two of the words.

Choice Box

A. past tense/present tense verbs	B. singular/plural nouns
C. antonyms	D. synonyms

fix   repair   bathing   billboard

_____ relationship

_____

_____

foolish   dwell   bathroom   wise

_____ relationship

_____

_____

forget   blame   blank   forgot

_____ relationship

_____

_____

geese   adventure   afterward   goose

_____ relationship

_____

_____

freeze   blast   froze   blaze

_____ relationship

_____

_____

Definitions

adventure: an exciting experience

afterward: at a later time

bathing: washing a body

bathroom: a room equipped for taking a bath or shower

billboard: a flat surface, usually outdoors, on which large advertisements are posted

blame: to hold responsible

blank: empty

blast: a sudden and violent gust of wind

blaze: a bright flame or fire

dwell: to live or stay as a permanent resident

fix: to repair; mend

foolish: unwise

forget: to fail to remember

forgot: failed to remember

freeze: to change from liquid to ice by loss of heat

froze: hardened into ice

geese: large web-footed swimming birds

goose: a web-footed swimming bird that is larger than a duck

repair: to restore to a good condition after damage

wise: intelligent

Circle the two words in each group that share a relationship shown in the choice box. Write the letter of the relationship. Then write a sentence using at least two of the words.

Choice Box

A. past tense/present tense verbs   B. singular/plural nouns

C. antonyms   D. synonyms

fret   bleed   worry   bless

_____ relationship

_____

_____

fry   blessing   fried   blew

_____ relationship

_____

_____

given   afterwards   blossum   taken

_____ relationship

_____

_____

gentleman   bloom   aid   gentlemen

_____ relationship

_____

_____

granddaughter   mend   grandson   mix

_____ relationship

_____

_____

Definitions

afterwards: at a later time

aid: to help

bleed: to lose blood

bless: to bestow good of any kind

blessing: bestowing good of any kind

blew: to move along, as by the wind

bloom: the flowering of a plant

blossom: the flower of a plant

fret: to feel or express worry

fried: cooked in a pan over heat, usually in oil

fry: to cook in a pan over heat, usually in oil

gentleman: a well-mannered man

gentlemen: well-mannered men

given: to present voluntarily and without expecting payment

granddaughter: a daughter of one's son or daughter

grandson: a son of one's son or daughter

mend: repair

mix: to combine

taken: to receive

worry: concern

Circle the two words in each group that share a relationship shown in the choice box. Write the letter of the relationship. Then write a sentence using at least two of the words.

Choice Box

A. past tense/present tense verbs	B. singular/plural nouns
C. antonyms	D. synonyms

go   aim   went   airy

_____ relationship

_____

_____

grandchild   address   grandchildren   admire

_____ relationship

_____

_____

giving   taking   ah   aged

_____ relationship

_____

_____

grape   Monday   grapes   unpleasant

_____ relationship

_____

_____

happiness   month   sadness   moo

_____ relationship

_____

_____

Definitions

address: the location of a place
admire: to regard with wonder, pleasure, or approval
aged: the length of time a being or thing has existed
ah: used as an exclamation of pain, surprise, or pity
aim: to point
airy: breezy
giving: presenting voluntarily and without expecting payment
go: to move, especially to or from something
grandchild: a child of one's son or daughter
grandchildren: children of one's son or daughter

grape: smooth-skinned fruit that grows on vines
grapes: fruits that grow on vines
happiness: cheerfulness
Monday: the second day of the week, following Sunday
month: any of the twelve parts into which the calendar year is divided
moo: the deep sound of a cow
sadness: unhappiness
taking: getting
unpleasant: bad
went: moved especially to or from something

Circle the two words in each group that share a relationship shown in the choice box. Write the letter of the relationship. Then write a sentence using at least two of the words.

Choice Box

A. past tense/present tense verbs   B. singular/plural nouns

C. antonyms   D. synonyms

hid   muddy   nap   hide

_____ relationship

_____

_____

host   mud   napkin   guest

_____ relationship

_____

_____

strange   murder   mule   odd

_____ relationship

_____

_____

hurried   mug   nail   hurry

_____ relationship

_____

_____

knife   mostly   motor   knives

_____ relationship

_____

_____

Definitions

guest: a person who spends some time at another person's home

hid: concealed from sight

hide: to conceal from sight

host: a person who entertains guests at home

hurried: moving or working rapidly

hurry: to move, proceed, or act with speed

knife: an instrument for cutting

knives: instruments for cutting

mostly: for the most part

motor: a small and powerful engine

mud: wet, soft earth

muddy: covered with mud

mug: a drinking cup

mule: a hybrid between a donkey and a horse

murder: the killing of another human being

nail: a piece of metal used with a hammer for holding pieces together

nap: to sleep for a short time

napkin: a small piece of cloth or paper for use in wiping the lips and fingers while eating

odd: different

strange: unusual

Circle the two words in each group that share a relationship
shown in the choice box. Write the letter of the relationship.
Then write a sentence using at least two of the words.

Choice Box

A. past tense/present tense verbs   B. singular/plural nouns

C. antonyms   D. synonyms

living   monkey   dying   mop

_____ relationship

_____

_____

leave   mount   mow   left

_____ relationship

_____

_____

hung   Mr.   hang   moose

_____ relationship

_____

_____

loaf   carload   loaves   eager

_____ relationship

_____

_____

married   morrow   marry   moss

_____ relationship

_____

_____

Definitions

carload: the amount carried by a car

dying: ceasing to live

eager: impatiently longing

hang: to attach a thing so that it is supported only from above

hung: attached a thing so that it is supported only from above

leave: to go out of or away from

left: went out

living: to have life

loaf: bread

loaves: breads

married: united in wedlock

marry: to wed

monkey: any mammal of the primate order

moose: a large, long-headed mammal in the deer family

mop: a bundle of absorbent material, fastened at the end of a stick or handle for washing floors

morrow: the next day

moss: a flowerless plant growing on moist ground or tree trunks

mount: to go up; climb

mow: to cut down grass or grain

Mr.: a title of respect used before a man's name (mister)

Circle the two words in each group that share a relationship shown in the choice box. Write the letter of the relationship. Then write a sentence using at least two of the words.

Choice Box

A. past tense/present tense verbs   B. singular/plural nouns

C. antonyms   D. synonyms

mouse   used   mice   weaken

_____ relationship

_____

_____

rear   swan   front   swat

_____ relationship

_____

_____

pea   valentine   wayside   peas

_____ relationship

_____

_____

punish   sweat   reward   swell

_____ relationship

_____

_____

sing   swallow   sword   sung

_____ relationship

_____

_____

Definitions

front: the part of anything that faces forward

mice: small rodents

mouse: a small rodent

pea: the round, edible seed of the legume family

peas: round, edible seeds of the legume family

punish: penalize; discipline

rear: the back of something

reward: something given for service or merit

sing: to perform a song

sung: carried a tune

swallow: gulp

swan: a stately water bird having a long, slender neck

swat: to hit; slap; smack

sweat: to perspire

swell: to grow in bulk

sword: a weapon with one end pointed and the other fixed in a handle

used: made use of

valentine: a message sent by one person to another on Valentine's Day

wayside: land next to a road, highway, or path

weaken: to make weak or weaker

Circle the two words in each group that share a relationship shown in the choice box. Write the letter of the relationship. Then write a sentence using at least two of the words.

Choice Box

A. past tense/present tense verbs	B. singular/plural nouns
C. antonyms	D. synonyms

peach   valuable   wax   peaches

_____ relationship

_____

_____

plain   fancy   milkman   eagle

_____ relationship

_____

_____

ponies   vase   pony   vegetable

_____ relationship

_____

_____

pop   swing   popped   switch

_____ relationship

_____

_____

sting   careful   stung   carriage

_____ relationship

_____

_____

Definitions

careful: cautious

carriage: a wheeled vehicle for carrying people, pulled by horses

eagle: a large, soaring bird of prey belonging to the hawk family

fancy: imagination or fantasy

milkman: a person who sells or delivers milk

peach: a soft juicy fruit containing a single seed

peaches: more than one peach

plain: dull, everyday

ponies: small horses

pony: a horse of any small type

pop: to make a short, quick, explosive sound

popped: made a short, quick, explosive sound

sting: a bite from a bee

stung: bitten by a bee

swing: to move to and fro

switch: what is used to turn on a device

valuable: priceless

vase: a container used to hold cut flowers

vegetable: any plant used as food

wax: a solid secreted by bees used in constructing their honeycomb

Circle the two words in each group that share a relationship shown in the choice box. Write the letter of the relationship. Then write a sentence using at least two of the words.

Choice Box

A. past tense/present tense verbs   B. singular/plural nouns

C. antonyms   D. synonyms

potato   velvet   potatoes   vessel

_____ relationship

_____

_____

pull   swift   swimming   push

_____ relationship

_____

_____

rub   swam   rubbed   swamped

_____ relationship

_____

_____

shake   ear   surely   shook

_____ relationship

_____

_____

shear   victory   sheared   washtub

_____ relationship

_____

_____

Definitions

ear: the organ of hearing in humans and animals

potato: a plant with round underground stems used as a vegetable

potatoes: more than one potato

pull: to draw toward oneself

push: to press against a thing with force in order to move it away

rub: to stroke

rubbed: polished

shake: to move with short, quick movements

shear: to remove by cutting or clipping with a sharp tool

sheared: removed by cutting or clipping with a sharp tool

shook: moved with short, quick movements

surely: absolutely, clearly

swam: to move through water using arms and legs

swamp: a tract of wet, spongy land

swift: moving or capable of moving with great speed

swimming: moving in water by using arms and legs

velvet: a thick, soft fabric

vessel: a craft for traveling on water, usually larger than a rowboat

victory: a win

washtub: a tub for use in washing clothes

Circle the two words in each group that share a relationship shown in the choice box. Write the letter of the relationship. Then write a sentence using at least two of the words.

Choice Box

A. past tense/present tense verbs	B. singular/plural nouns
C. antonyms	D. synonyms

shiny   violet   dull   visitor

_____ relationship

_____

_____

taught   fill   teach   fifth

_____ relationship

_____

_____

sink   wag   float   wagon

_____ relationship

_____

_____

slid   pearl   slide   waterproof

_____ relationship

_____

_____

smile   frown   wave   carelessness

_____ relationship

_____

_____

Definitions

carelessness: not paying enough attention to what one does

dull: not sharp

fifth: the next one after the fourth

fill: to make full

float: to rest or remain on the surface of a liquid

frown: scowl

pearl: a smooth, rounded bead formed within the shells of certain mollusks

shiny: bright or glossy in appearance

sink: to fall below the surface or to the bottom

slid: moved along in continuous contact with a smooth or slippery surface

slide: to move along in continuous

contact with a smooth or slippery surface

smile: a facial expression indicating pleasure, favor, or amusement

taught: gave instruction in

teach: give instruction in

violet: a low, leafy plant with flowers

visitor: a person who visits

wag: to move from side to side

wagon: any of various kinds of four-wheeled vehicles designed to be pulled or having its own motor

waterproof: closed to water

wave: a signal made with the hand

Circle the two words in each group that share a relationship shown in the choice box. Write the letter of the relationship. Then write a sentence using at least two of the words.

Choice Box

A. past tense/present tense verbs	B. singular/plural nouns
C. antonyms	D. synonyms

spend   upstairs   spent   weapon

_____ relationship

_____

_____

sunny   shady   finger   finish

_____ relationship

_____

_____

stole   careless   steal   carpenter

_____ relationship

_____

_____

stripe   card   cape   stripes

_____ relationship

_____

_____

sunrise   firing   sunset   fist

_____ relationship

_____

_____

Definitions

cape: shawl, poncho

card: a piece of paper printed with a greeting

careless: not paying enough attention to what one does

carpenter: person who builds or repairs wooden structures

finger: any of the end members of the hand, one other than the thumb

finish: to bring something to an end

firing: to set on fire

fist: the hand closed tightly, with the fingers doubled into the palm

shady: shadowy

spend: to pay out

spent: paid out

steal: to take the property of another without permission

stole: took the property of another without permission

stripe: a long, narrow band of a different color from the rest of the thing

stripes: long, narrow bands of different colors

sunny: plenty of sunshine

sunrise: the rise of the sun above the horizon in the morning

sunset: the setting of the sun below the horizon in the evening

upstairs: up the stairs; to floor

weapon : any instrument used to attack or defend

Circle the two words in each group that share a relationship shown in the choice box. Write the letter of the relationship. Then write a sentence using at least two of the words.

Choice Box

A. past tense/present tense verbs	B. singular/plural nouns
C. antonyms	D. synonyms

swear   fits   flags   swore

_____ relationship

_____

_____

sweater   slow   quick   sweetness

_____ relationship

_____

_____

sweep   flake   swept   flame

_____ relationship

_____

_____

sweet   flap   flash   sour

_____ relationship

_____

_____

tear   fifty   tore   file

_____ relationship

_____

_____

Definitions

fifty: ten times five

file: a system to arrange papers in order

fits: the proper size and shape

flag: a piece of cloth, used as the symbol of a nation, state, or organization

flake: peel off

flame: fire

flap: to swing or sway back and forth loosely

flash: a brief, sudden burst of bright light

quick: occurring with promptness

slow: moving or proceeding with little or less than usual speed

sour: tart

swear: to make a solemn declaration

sweater: a knitted jacket

sweep: to remove dirt with a broom

sweet: having the taste of sugar or honey

sweetness: the taste of sugar or honey

swept: removed dirt with a broom

swore: made a solemn oath

tear: to pull apart in pieces

tore: pulled apart in pieces

Circle the two words in each group that share a relationship shown in the choice box. Write the letter of the relationship. Then write a sentence using at least two of the words.

Choice Box

A. past tense/present tense verbs   B. singular/plural nouns

C. antonyms   D. synonyms

teeth   fife   tooth   fifteen

_____ relationship

_____

_____

threw   fail   throw   faraway

_____ relationship

_____

_____

unfold   fold   fib   fiddle

_____ relationship

_____

_____

wake   February   woke   fellow

_____ relationship

_____

_____

unfriendly   far-off   friendly   fell

_____ relationship

_____

_____

Definitions

fail: be unsuccessful

faraway: remote, distant

far-off: very far away in space or time

February: the second month of the year with 28 days or 29 days in leap years

fell: to drop down

fellow: a man or boy

fib: a small lie

fiddle: a musical instrument

fife: a high-pitched flute

fifteen: ten plus five

fold: to bend cloth or paper over upon itself

friendly: showing friendship

teeth: the hard bodies attached in a row to each jaw

threw: project from the hand by a forward motion

throw: to project from the hand by a forward motion

tooth: one of the hard bodies attached in a row to each jaw

unfold: to open out

unfriendly: not friendly

wake: arise from sleep

woke: became awake

Circle the two words in each group that share a relationship shown in the choice box. Write the letter of the relationship. Then write a sentence using at least two of the words.

Choice Box

A. past tense/present tense verbs	B. singular/plural nouns
C. antonyms	D. synonyms

watchman   shoot   vote   shot

_____ relationship

_____

_____

unhurt   fence   hurt   fever

_____ relationship

_____

_____

upper   breakfast   upset   meal

_____ relationship

_____

_____

upside   cash   charge   mistake

_____ relationship

_____

_____

vine   shine   watermelon   shone

_____ relationship

_____

_____

Definitions

breakfast: the first meal of the day

cash: money

charge: to pay with a credit card

fence: a barrier around a yard

fever: a high body temperature

hurt: injury

meal: the food eaten at breakfast, lunch, or supper

mistake: an error

shine: to glow with light

shone: glowed with light

shoot: to fire a weapon

shot: discharged a weapon

unhurt : not injured

upper: higher

upset: disturbed

upside: the upper side

vine: any plant having a long, slender stem that trails on the ground or climbs

vote: a formal expression of choice

watchman: a person who keeps guard over a building to protect it

watermelon: a large fruit having a green rind and a sweet, juicy, red pulp

Circle the two words in each group that share a relationship shown in the choice box. Write the letter of the relationship. Then write a sentence using at least two of the words.

Choice Box

A. past tense/present tense verbs	B. singular/plural nouns
C. antonyms	D. synonyms

waken   smart   waist   clever

_____ relationship

_____

_____

walnut   waste   slipped   slip

_____ relationship

_____

_____

weak   nice   moving   naughty

_____ relationship

_____

_____

weakness   movie   useful   movies

_____ relationship

_____

_____

obey   coat   wedding   cloak

_____ relationship

_____

_____

Definitions

clever: mentally bright

cloak: cape

coat: a covering used to protect the body

movie: motion picture

movies: motion pictures

moving: to pass from one place to another

naughty: disobedient

nice: pleasing

obey: to follow commands

slip: to move smoothly or easily; glide; slide

slipped: moved smoothly or easily; glide; slide

smart: intelligent

useful: helpful

waist: the part of the human body between the ribs and the hips

waken: to stop sleeping

walnut: an edible nut

waste: garbage

weak: not strong

weakness: lack of strength

wedding: to marry another person in a ceremony

Circle the two words in each group that share a relationship shown in the choice box. Write the letter of the relationship. Then write a sentence using at least two of the words.

Choice Box

A. past tense/present tense verbs	B. singular/plural nouns
C. antonyms	D. synonyms

whip   feast   whipped   feather

_____ relationship

_____

_____

willing   basket   bat   unwilling

_____ relationship

_____

_____

wrap   bathe   wrapped   absent

_____ relationship

_____

_____

winner   bath   batch   loser

_____ relationship

_____

_____

wring   battle   bay   wrung

_____ relationship

_____

_____

Definitions

absent: missing

basket: a container made of flexible material woven together

bat: the wooden club used in baseball to strike the ball

batch: a quantity taken together

bath: a washing of something

bathe: to immerse in water for cleansing

battle: a fight

bay: a body of water with a shoreline

feast: a large meal

feather: one of the light, flat growths forming the principal covering of birds

loser: a person who loses

unwilling: against

whip: to beat (eggs, cream)

whipped: beaten

willing: agreeable

winner: a person or thing that wins

wrap: to enclose in something

wrapped: enclosed in something

wring: to twist forcibly

wrung: twisted forcibly

SECTION 2
Classifications Defined

Contractions are words that are shortened forms of two combined words. Contractions always have an apostrophe.

		Contractions
they are	⟶	they're
she will	⟶	she'll
do not	⟶	don't

Pronouns are words used as replacements or substitutes for nouns.

Nouns		**Pronouns**
Theo	⟶	he
flower	⟶	it
students	⟶	they

Homophones are words that sound the same but have diffferent spellings and meanings.

flower	⟶	flour
hare	⟶	hair
tale	⟶	tail

Compound words are words made by joining two words.

fire + man	⟶	fireman
pan + cake	⟶	pancake
bed + room	⟶	bedroom

SECTION 2

Circle the two words in each group that share a relationship shown in the choice box. Write the letter of the relationship. Then write a sentence using at least two of the words.

Choice Box

E. contractions	F. compound words
G. homophones	H. pronouns

blindfold   liver   lively   bathtub

_____ relationship

_____

_____

joy   shouldn't   jaw   she's

_____ relationship

_____

_____

all   crowded   crow   these

_____ relationship

_____

_____

burn   but   bunch   butt

_____ relationship

_____

_____

coconut   birthday   cobbler   anyway

_____ relationship

_____

_____

Definitions

all: the whole quantity

anyway: in any case

bathtub: a tub to bathe in

birthday: the anniversary of a birth

blindfold: a cloth that covers the eyes to prevent sight

bunch: a connected group

burn: result of fire

but: yet

butt: the thicker end considered as a bottom

cobbler: a deep-dish fruit pie with a top crust

coconut: the large, hardshelled seed of the coconut palm

crow: a large black bird

crowded: persons gathered closely together

jaw: either of two bones forming the mouth

jay: any of several noisy birds of the crow family

lively: full of life, active

liver: an organ in the body

she's: she is

shouldn't: should not

these: used to indicate people or things

Circle the two words in each group that share a relationship shown in the choice box. Write the letter of the relationship. Then write a sentence using at least two of the words.

Choice Box

E. contractions	F. compound words
G. homophones	H. pronouns

anyone   breath   breast   each

_____ relationship

_____

_____

background   collar   college   anyhow

_____ relationship

_____

_____

ceiling   needn't   jelly   he'll

_____ relationship

_____

_____

dancer   bedbug   dame   battleship

_____ relationship

_____

_____

beach   bundle   beech   bunny

_____ relationship

_____

_____

Definitions

anyhow: in any way whatever
anyone: any person at all
background: the parts, as of a scene, situated in the rear
battleship: warships that are heavily armored and equipped with armament
beach: an expanse of sand or pebbles along a shore
bedbug: a flat, wingless, blood-sucking insect that infests houses and beds
beech: a tree having a smooth gray bark
breast: the chest
breath: the air inhaled and exhaled in respiration
bundle: several objects bound together

bunny: a young rabbit
ceiling: the overhead surface of a room
collar: the part of a shirt that circles the neckline
college: a school of higher learning
dame: the official title of a wife of a knight
dancer: a person who dances
each: one by one
he'll: he will
jelly: a sweet spread for bread and toast
needn't: need not

Circle the two words in each group that share a relationship shown in the choice box. Write the letter of the relationship. Then write a sentence using at least two of the words.

Choice Box

E. contractions	F. compound words
G. homophones	H. pronouns

knee   bedspread   kitty   bobwhite

_____ relationship

_____

_____

butter   wrote   button   rote

_____ relationship

_____

_____

bedroom   comfort   bookcase   comic

_____ relationship

_____

_____

bottle   bounce   everything   few

_____ relationship

_____

_____

bowl   bow-wow   sight   site

_____ relationship

_____

_____

Definitions

bedroom: a room used for sleeping

bedspread: an outer covering for a bed

bobwhite: any of several American quail

bookcase: a set of shelves for books

bottle: a portable container for holding liquids

bounce: to spring back from a surface in a lively manner

bowl: a deep, round dish

bow-wow: the bark of a dog

butter: a spread for bread

button: fastener

comfort: to help

comic: funnyman

everything: all

few: not many but more than one

kitty: a kitten

knee: the joint of the leg that allows for movement

rote: routine

sight: vision

wrote: formed letters or words on paper

site: the location of a town or building

Circle the two words in each group that share a relationship shown in the choice box. Write the letter of the relationship. Then write a sentence using at least two of the words.

Choice Box

E. contractions	F. compound words
G. homophones	H. pronouns

lives   blackbird   lit   beehive

_____ relationship

_____

_____

blackberry   lion   haircut   lip

_____ relationship

_____

_____

broke   dew   bubble   due

_____ relationship

_____

_____

knit   broadcast   kneel   boyhood

_____ relationship

_____

_____

aunt   bush   ant   bus

_____ relationship

_____

_____

Definitions

ant: any of numerous social insects

aunt: the sister of one's father or mother

beehive: a home constructed for bees

blackberry: a wild berry fruit that is very dark purple when ripe

blackbird: any of several birds having black feathers

boyhood: the years of being a boy

broadcast: to throw over an area

broke: smashed into parts

bubble: a circle of gas, soap, or gum

bus: a large motor vehicle equipped with seats for passengers

bush: a low plant with many branches

dew: water droplets

due: having reached the date for payment or expiration

haircut: the act of cutting hair

kneel: to go down or rest on the knees

knit: to make clothing with yarn

lion: a large, wild cat living in Africa and Asia

lip: the two fleshy parts forming the mouth

lit: something that is visible by light

lives: to be alive

Circle the two words in each group that share a relationship shown in the choice box. Write the letter of the relationship. Then write a sentence using at least two of the words.

Choice Box

E. contractions	F. compound words
G. homophones	H. pronouns

housewife   clang   otherwise   citizen

_____ relationship

_____

_____

them   butcher   busy   us

_____ relationship

_____

_____

chop   chorus   campfire   housetop

_____ relationship

_____

_____

bushel   lesson   brick   lessen

_____ relationship

_____

_____

cleaner   bedtime   clerk   beefsteak

_____ relationship

_____

_____

Definitions

bedtime: the time a person goes to bed
beefsteak: a cut of beef
brick: a block of clay hardened by drying
bushel: a unit of dry measure
busy: active
butcher: a person who cuts meat
campfire: an outdoor fire for warmth or cooking
chop: to cut with a quick series of blows
chorus: a group of persons singing together
citizen: a legal resident of a country
clang: a loud sound produced by a large bell

cleaner: less dirt than before
clerk: a person who keeps records
housetop: the top of a house
housewife: a married woman who manages her household
lessen: to become less
lesson: assignment
otherwise: under other circumstances
them: any people or animals
us: ourselves

Circle the two words in each group that share a relationship shown in the choice box. Write the letter of the relationship. Then write a sentence using at least two of the words.

Choice Box

| E. contractions | F. compound words |
| G. homophones | H. pronouns |

cell   burst   sell   bury

_____ relationship

_____

_____

mailman   climb   haystack   cliff

_____ relationship

_____

_____

clothing   necktie   cloudy   neighborhood

_____ relationship

_____

_____

his   bull   bulb   it

_____ relationship

_____

_____

headache   cob   mailbox   coal

_____ relationship

_____

_____

Definitions

bulb: an electric lamp
bull: the male of certain animals
burst: to break open with sudden violence
bury: to put in the ground and cover with earth
cell: a small room, as in a prison
cliff: a high steep face of a rock
climb: to go up
clothing: coverings for the body
cloudy: the sky covered with clouds
coal: a natural material used as a fuel
cob: a corncob
haystack: a stack of hay

headache: a pain in the head
his: that belonging to him
it: used to represent a person, animal, or thing
mailbox: a box in which mail is placed for pickup and delivery by the post office
mailman: a mail carrier
necktie: a band of fabric worn around the neck
neighborhood: the area around a house
sell: to transfer goods for money

Circle the two words in each group that share a relationship shown in the choice box. Write the letter of the relationship. Then write a sentence using at least two of the words.

Choice Box

E. contractions	F. compound words
G. homophones	H. pronouns

bother   mine   wildcat   me

_____ relationship

_____

_____

dare   rattlesnake   dandy   outlaw

_____ relationship

_____

_____

couldn't   kitchen   kid   wouldn't

_____ relationship

_____

_____

crab   kernel   crack   colonel

_____ relationship

_____

_____

conductor   outfit   cone   coffeepot

_____ relationship

_____

_____

Definitions

bother: annoy
coffeepot: a container used to make coffee
colonel: an officer in the army
conductor: a leader
cone: a shape whose base is a circle and whose sides taper up to a point
couldn't: could not
crab: a sea creature
crack: to break without separating
dandy: excellent
dare: to have the necessary courage for something
kernel: the softer part in the shell of a nut
kid: a child

kitchen: a room used for cooking
me: used by a speaker in talking about himself or herself
mine: something that belongs to me
outfit: clothes
outlaw : bandit
rattlesnake: a pit viper that has a tail that makes a buzzing sound
wildcat: a cat that is not a pet
wouldn't: would not
rattlesnake: a pit viper that has a tail that makes a buzzing sound

Circle the two words in each group that share a relationship shown in the choice box. Write the letter of the relationship. Then write a sentence using at least two of the words.

Choice Box

E. contractions	F. compound words
G. homophones	H. pronouns

cradle   navel   cramps   naval

_____ relationship

_____

_____

daytime   darling   doorbell   dart

_____ relationship

_____

_____

crush   wreak   reek   crust

_____ relationship

_____

_____

cardboard   date   cupboard   dash

_____ relationship

_____

_____

dear   brook   deer   broom

_____ relationship

_____

_____

Definitions

brook: a small stream of fresh water

broom: a tool for sweeping

cardboard: a thin, stiff pasteboard used for boxes

cradle: a small bed for a baby that rocks

cramps: sudden, severe pains

crush: to mash or crunch

crust: the surface of a loaf of bread

cupboard: a closet with shelves for dishes

darling: one dearly loved

dart: to race away

dash: to chase

date: a particular month, day, and year

daytime: the time between sunrise and sunset

dear: loved

deer: hoofed animals with antlers

doorbell: a chime rung by someone outside the door

naval: belonging to the navy

navel: the mark on the stomach where the umbilical cord was attached

reek: to have a strong, unpleasant smell

wreak: to cause

Circle the two words in each group that share a relationship shown in the choice box. Write the letter of the relationship. Then write a sentence using at least two of the words.

Choice Box

E. contractions   F. compound words

G. homophones   H. pronouns

doorknob   cent   dressmaker   cereal

_____ relationship

_____

_____

brush   we   broken   I

_____ relationship

_____

_____

jail   everyday   jar   doorstep

_____ relationship

_____

_____

boss   he   boot   this

_____ relationship

_____

_____

daddy   flashlight   dancing   fisherman

_____ relationship

_____

_____

Definitions

boot: a shoe to protect the foot from water
boss: manager
broken: smashed into pieces
brush: a tool used for painting
cent: a penny
cereal: a grain eaten at breakfast
daddy: a dad
dancing: to move one's feet and body to music
doorknob: the handle used to open or close a door
doorstep: a step leading from the ground to a door
dressmaker: a person who makes clothes
everyday: daily

fisherman: a person who fishes
flashlight: a small lamp powered by batteries
he: the male person
I: used to refer to oneself
jail: a prison
jar: a glass container used to store food
this: used to refer to a thing
we: ourselves

Circle the two words in each group that share a relationship shown in the choice box. Write the letter of the relationship. Then write a sentence using at least two of the words.

Choice Box

E. contractions	F. compound words
G. homophones	H. pronouns

flour   won   flower   wonderful

_____ relationship

_____

_____

hayfield   sickness   dad   footprint

_____ relationship

_____

_____

who   bucket   herself   buckle

_____ relationship

_____

_____

juice   hayfield   worth   forehead

_____ relationship

_____

_____

hers   cruel   any   crown

_____ relationship

_____

_____

Definitions

any: some
bucket: pail
buckle: a clasp used to fasten one end of a belt to the other end
crown: headgear worn by a monarch
cruel: willfully causing pain to others
dad: a father
flour: the finely ground powder of grain used in baking
flower: the blossom of a plant
football: a game in which two opposing teams defend goals at opposite ends of a field
footprint: an impression of the sole of a person's foot

forehead: the part of the face above the eyebrows
hayfield: a field where grass is grown for making into hay
hers: belonging to her
herself: the one identical with her
juice: liquid from a fruit
sickness: illness
who: refers to a person or persons
won: to finish first in a game
wonderful: great
worth: having a value

Circle the two words in each group that share a relationship shown in the choice box. Write the letter of the relationship. Then write a sentence using at least two of the words.

Choice Box

E. contractions	F. compound words
G. homophones	H. pronouns

goldfish   gunpowder   locomotive   log

_____ relationship

_____

_____

hay   joyous   wooden   hey

_____ relationship

_____

_____

joyful   firearm   jug   grasshopper

_____ relationship

_____

_____

Greece   cracker   canoe   grease

_____ relationship

_____

_____

outward   firecracker   jam   January

_____ relationship

_____

_____

Definitions

canoe: slender, open boats using paddles to move
cracker: a thin, crisp biscuit
firearm: a gun
firecracker: a small explosive used to make a noise, as during a celebration
goldfish: a small fish often kept in fishbowls
grasshopper: an insect having hind legs for jumping
grease: the melted fat of animals
Greece: a country in Europe
gunpowder: ammunition
hay: grass cut and dried for use as food for farm animals
hey: hello

jam: to fill too full
January: the first month of the year
joyful: glad
joyous: happy
jug: container
locomotive: an engine used to move trains
log: a piece of a cut tree
outward: directed toward the outside
wooden: made of wood

Circle the two words in each group that share a relationship shown in the choice box. Write the letter of the relationship. Then write a sentence using at least two of the words.

Choice Box

E. contractions	F. compound words
G. homophones	H. pronouns

groan   cowboy   grown   cozy

_____ relationship

_____

_____

handwriting   coin   downtown   June

_____ relationship

_____

_____

hart   honk   heart   hoop

_____ relationship

_____

_____

downstairs   boiler   grandstand   clap

_____ relationship

_____

_____

hasn't   kite   aren't   cave

_____ relationship

_____

_____

Definitions

aren't: are not
boiler: a tank used to heat water
cave: a hole in a mountain
clap: to strike one's hands against one another
coin: a piece of metal stamped and used as money
cowboy: a man who herds and tends cattle on a ranch
cozy: snugly warm and comfortable
downstairs: down the stairs
downtown: the main business section of a city
grandstand: the main seating area of a stadium

groan: a low, mournful sound uttered in pain
grown: increased in size
handwriting: writing done with a pen or pencil in the hand
hart: a male red deer
hasn't: has not
heart: an organ that circulates blood in the body
honk: the cry of a goose
hoop: a ring of metal, wood, or plastic
June: the sixth month of the year, containing 30 days
kite: a light frame covered with some thin material, to be flown in the wind at the end of a long string

Circle the two words in each group that share a relationship
shown in the choice box. Write the letter of the relationship.
Then write a sentence using at least two of the words.

Choice Box

E. contractions	F. compound words
G. homophones	H. pronouns

hardship   cocoon   coffee   homesick

_____ relationship

_____

_____

bridge   yourselves   bride   her

_____ relationship

_____

_____

coach   hardware   clump   henhouse

_____ relationship

_____

_____

jockey   I'd   jig   he's

_____ relationship

_____

_____

badge   hillside   bacon   highway

_____ relationship

_____

_____

Definitions

bacon: cured pork
badge: an emblem or pin
bride: a newly married woman
bridge: a structure across a river or road
clump: a small, close group
coach: a person who trains an athlete or a team
cocoon: the silky envelope spun by the larvae of many insects
coffee: a beverage consisting of roasted ground coffee beans
hardship: suffering
hardware: tools
henhouse: a shelter for chickens
her: she
he's: he is or he has
highway: a main road

hillside: the side of a hill
homesick: a longing for home or family while away from them
I'd: I would or I had
jig: a dance
jockey: a person who rides horses professionally in races
yourselves: used in place of you as a group

Circle the two words in each group that share a relationship shown in the choice box. Write the letter of the relationship. Then write a sentence using at least two of the words.

Choice Box

E. contractions   F. compound words

G. homophones   H. pronouns

those   buffalo   himself   buggy

_____ relationship

_____

_____

bag   honeymoon   badly   hilltop

_____ relationship

_____

_____

hi   wreck   high   bullet

_____ relationship

_____

_____

honeybee   click   bake   godmother

_____ relationship

_____

_____

I'm   cellar   I've   jerk

_____ relationship

_____

_____

Definitions

badly: in an incorrect way

bag: a container that can be closed at the top

bake: to cook in an oven

buffalo: a large wild oxen

buggy: a light, four-wheeled, horse-drawn carriage with a single seat

bullet: ammunition

cellar: an underground storage for food

click: a slight, sharp sound

godmother: a woman who serves as sponsor for a child at baptism

hilltop: the top of a hill

himself: that one identical with him

hi: a greeting

high: tall

honeybee: any bee that collects and stores honey

honeymoon: a vacation taken by a newly married couple

I'm: I am

I've: I have

jerk: a sudden movement

those: refers to people or things

wreck: a serious accident

Circle the two words in each group that share a relationship
shown in the choice box. Write the letter of the relationship.
Then write a sentence using at least two of the words.

Choice Box

E. contractions	F. compound words
G. homophones	H. pronouns

hoof   manor   hook   manner

_____ relationship

_____

_____

its   bow   that   broad

_____ relationship

_____

_____

hop   intense   honey   intents

_____ relationship

_____

_____

horseback   christen   automobile   circus

_____ relationship

_____

_____

isle   aisle   cover   cowardly

_____ relationship

_____

_____

Definitions

aisle: a walkway between sections of seats in a classroom
automobile: car
bow: to bend or curve downward
broad: large
christen: baptize
circus: a traveling group that presents entertainment featuring clowns and animals
cover: wrapping
cowardly: timid
honey: a sweet fluid produced by bees
hoof: the hard covering protecting the ends of the foot in certain animals, like the horse
hook: a curved piece of metal

for catching, pulling, or holding
hop: move by leaping with all feet off the ground
horseback: the back of a horse
intense: a strong emotion
intents: purposes
isle: a small island
its: belonging to it
manner: behavior
manor: the main house of a lord
that: used to indicate a thing

Circle the two words in each group that share a relationship shown in the choice box. Write the letter of the relationship. Then write a sentence using at least two of the words.

Choice Box

| E. contractions | F. compound words |
| G. homophones | H. pronouns |

she'll   joking   she'd   join

_____ relationship

_____

_____

claw   lookout   cigarette   jellyfish

_____ relationship

_____

_____

jolly   that's   liking   haven't

_____ relationship

_____

_____

everywhere   kindness   journey   eyebrow

_____ relationship

_____

_____

linen   what's   lock   who'd

_____ relationship

_____

_____

Definitions

cigarette: a roll of finely cut tobacco used for smoking
claw: a sharp nail on the foot of an animal
everywhere: in every place
eyebrow: the hair growing above the eye
haven't: have not
jellyfish: free-swimming marine animals having a soft body
join: connect
joking: something said or done to make someone laugh
jolly: happy
journey: a trip
kindness: helpfulness
liking: favoring

linen: fabric woven from flax yarns
lock: a device for securing a door
lookout: the act of keeping watch
she'd: she would or she had
she'll: she will
that's: that has or that is
what's: what does or what is
who'd: who would

Circle the two words in each group that share a relationship
shown in the choice box. Write the letter of the relationship.
Then write a sentence using at least two of the words.

Choice Box

E. contractions	F. compound words
G. homophones	H. pronouns

maypole   kick   fireworks   kettle

_____ relationship

_____

_____

kill   they'll   kindly   they're

_____ relationship

_____

_____

hairpin   kiss   fireplace   kingdom

_____ relationship

_____

_____

kitten   hadn't   lace   he'd

_____ relationship

_____

_____

buttercup   knot   bumblebee   knock

_____ relationship

_____

_____

Definitions

bumblebee: any of several large, hairy social bees

buttercup: a wildflower with yellow blossoms

fireplace: a structure for keeping a fire

fireworks: explosive displays with lights and noises

hadn't: had not

hairpin: a pin used to hold women's hair in place

he'd: he had or he would

kettle: a pot used for cooking

kick: to strike with the foot

kill: to cause the death of

kindly: kindhearted

kingdom: a government having a king or queen as its leader

kiss: to touch with the lips

kitten: a young cat

knock: to strike a sounding blow with anything hard, especially on a door,

knot: a cord or rope tied in a loop

lace: a cord used to draw and tie together, as a shoe

maypole: a tall pole, decorated with flowers and ribbons, around which people dance during May Day celebrations

they'll: they will

they're: they are

Circle the two words in each group that share a relationship shown in the choice box. Write the letter of the relationship. Then write a sentence using at least two of the words.

Choice Box

E. contractions	F. compound words
G. homophones	H. pronouns

levee   caller   bud   levy

_____ relationship

_____

_____

here's   limb   we'd   lily

_____ relationship

_____

_____

boxcar   ladies   bookkeeper   ladder

_____ relationship

_____

_____

links　　　　　　bun　　　　　　bump　　　　　　lynx

_____ relationship

_____

_____

him　　　　　　wool　　　　　　woods　　　　　　she

_____ relationship

_____

_____

Definitions

bookkeeper: accountant
boxcar: a completely enclosed freight car
bud: a sprout or a bloom
bump: to collide with
bun: bread rolls
caller: a person that calls
here's: here is
him: the male person
ladder: a tool used for climbing up or down
ladies: women who are polite
levee: a dam
levy: a tax
lily: a flowering plant
limb: a part of a body, as a leg
links: connections

lynx: a wildcat
she: referring to a female
we'd: we had, we should, or we would
woods: a forest
wool: a fabric used for warmth

Circle the two words in each group that share a relationship shown in the choice box. Write the letter of the relationship. Then write a sentence using at least two of the words.

Choice Box

E. contractions	F. compound words
G. homophones	H. pronouns

lizard   load   sunflower   bluebird

_____ relationship

_____

_____

loan   wipe   lone   wit

_____ relationship

_____

_____

loop   blackboard   loose   blueberry

_____ relationship

_____

_____

lyre   breathe   liar   breeze

_____ relationship

_____

_____

midnight   cannon   blacksmith   clip

_____ relationship

_____

_____

Definitions

blackboard: smooth, hard material to write on with chalk

blacksmith: a person who makes horseshoes

blueberry: the edible, usually bluish berry of various shrubs

bluebird: a songbird with blue feathers

breathe: inhale and exhale air

breeze: a wind

cannon: a mounted gun

clip: to cut

liar: a person who tells lies

lizard: a scaly reptile

load: anything put in or on something for carrying

loan: the temporary use of something

lone: being alone

loop: a circle

loose: baggy

lyre: a musical instrument

midnight: twelve o'clock at night

sunflower: a plant that has yellow flower heads and edible seeds

wipe: to rub lightly with a cloth, towel, paper, or the hand

wit: humor

Circle the two words in each group that share a relationship shown in the choice box. Write the letter of the relationship. Then write a sentence using at least two of the words.

Choice Box

E. contractions	F. compound words
G. homophones	H. pronouns

calf   most   woodpecker   myself

_____ relationship

_____

_____

junk   grandmother   keen   gooseberry

_____ relationship

_____

_____

mustard   hood   honor   mustered

_____ relationship

_____

_____

wink   grandfather   wing   gingerbread

_____ relationship

_____

_____

clown   elsewhere   clover   newspaper

_____ relationship

_____

_____

Definitions

calf: the young of a cow
clover: a plant in the pea family
clown: a comic performer as in a circus
elsewhere: somewhere else
gingerbread: a type of cake flavored with ginger and molasses
gooseberry: the edible fruit of certain shrubs
grandfather: the father of one's father or mother
grandmother: the mother of one's father or mother
honor: honesty
hood: a soft covering for the head and neck
junk: garbage

keen: having great mental ability
most: best thing
mustard: a paste prepared from ground mustard seeds
mustered: came together; gathered
myself: me
newspaper: a daily or weekly publication containing news
wing: a limb on most birds used for flying
wink: to close and open one or both eyes quickly
woodpecker: a climbing bird with a bill that hammers into wood in search of insects

Circle the two words in each group that share a relationship shown in the choice box. Write the letter of the relationship. Then write a sentence using at least two of the words.

Choice Box

| E. contractions | F. compound words |
| G. homophones | H. pronouns |

mown   woolen   moan   wore

_____ relationship

_____

_____

nightgown   cluck   club   nevermore

_____ relationship

_____

_____

none   nothing   youngster   yesterday

_____ relationship

_____

_____

cloth   friendship   closet   moonlight

_____ relationship

_____

_____

write   right   brass   bread

_____ relationship

_____

_____

Definitions

brass: a metal alloy consisting mainly of copper and zinc

bread: a baked food made of flour

closet: an area for storing clothing

cloth: a fabric

club: a heavy stick used as a weapon

cluck: the cry of a hen

friendship: companionship

moan: complaint

moonlight: the light of the moon

mown: cut down

nevermore: never again

nightgown: a loose gown worn in bed

none: no one

nothing: not anything

woolen: wool cloth or clothing

wore: carried on the body as a covering

right: correct

write: to trace or form letters on paper

yesterday: the day before this day

youngster: a young person

Circle the two words in each group that share a relationship shown in the choice box. Write the letter of the relationship. Then write a sentence using at least two of the words.

Choice Box

| E. contractions | F. compound words |
| G. homophones | H. pronouns |

nowhere   youth   one   yell

_____ relationship

_____

_____

churn   outdoors   Christmas   ourselves

_____ relationship

_____

_____

you'd   jump   you'll   junior

_____ relationship

_____

_____

hale   writing   hail   wren

_____ relationship

_____

_____

comb   grapefruit   colored   outline

_____ relationship

_____

_____

Definitions

Christmas: a holiday celebrated on December 25th
churn: a large milk can
colored: having color
comb: a toothed strip used for arranging the hair
grapefruit: a large citrus fruit
hail: to greet
hale: healthy
jump: to leap
junior: younger
nowhere: not anywhere
one: single
ourselves: those people in the same group
outdoors: in the open air
outline: the drawn shape of an object

wren: a small songbird
writing: tracing or forming letters on paper
yell: shout
you'd: you had or you would
you'll: you will
youth: characteristics of one who is young

Circle the two words in each group that share a relationship shown in the choice box. Write the letter of the relationship. Then write a sentence using at least two of the words.

Choice Box

E. contractions	F. compound words
G. homophones	H. pronouns

peak   boom   boo   peek

_____ relationship

_____

_____

peppermint   coming   pineapple   clay

_____ relationship

_____

_____

wound   heal   bum   heel

_____ relationship

_____

_____

carrot   chip   caret   choice

_____ relationship

_____

_____

stair   workman   stare   worm

_____ relationship

_____

_____

Definitions

boo: a sound used to startle or frighten

boom: a loud sound

bum: a person who does not work and lives off of others

caret: a mark (^) made where something should be added in written text

carrot: the orange root of a plant, eaten raw or cooked

chip: to break apart into small pieces

choice: selection

clay: a natural earthy material

coming: move toward a person or place

heal: to make healthy

heel: the back part of the human foot

peak: the pointed top of a mountain

peek: to look or glance quickly

peppermint: an herb of the mint family

pineapple: the edible, juicy fruit of a tropical plant

stair: one of a set of steps for going from one level to another

stare: to look at intently

workman: a male worker

worm: a long, slender, soft-bodied, legless animal

wound: an injury

Circle the two words in each group that share a relationship shown in the choice box. Write the letter of the relationship. Then write a sentence using at least two of the words.

Choice Box

E. contractions	F. compound words
G. homophones	H. pronouns

we've   joke   likely   can't

_____ relationship

_____

_____

warn   cries   crumb   worn

_____ relationship

_____

_____

who'll   limp   lime   they've

_____ relationship

_____

_____

use   yonder   ewes   crumble

_____ relationship

_____

_____

we're   who's   juicy   July

_____ relationship

_____

_____

Definitions

can't: cannot
cries: to utter sounds, especially of suffering, usually with tears
crumb: a small particle or portion of anything
crumble: to break into crumbs
ewes: female sheep
joke: something said or done to cause laughter
juicy: full of juice
July: the seventh month of the year, containing 31 days
likely: probable
lime: a green citrus fruit
limp: to walk unsteadily
they've: they have
use: to work with
warn: to give notice

we're: we are
we've: we have
who'll: we will
who's: who is or who has
worn: to have on the body
yonder: over there

Circle the two words in each group that share a relationship shown in the choice box. Write the letter of the relationship. Then write a sentence using at least two of the words.

Choice Box

| E. contractions | F. compound words |
| G. homophones | H. pronouns |

throne   yarn   worst   thrown

_____ relationship

_____

_____

windmill   much   my   calendar

_____ relationship

_____

_____

yolk   toe   worse   tow

_____ relationship

_____

_____

judge   they'd   joy   you've

_____ relationship

_____

_____

male   wolf   mail   witch

_____ relationship

_____

_____

Definitions

calendar: a table with the days of each month and week in a year

joy: the emotion of great happiness

judge: a person appointed to decide a contest

mail: letters and packages that are sent or delivered by means of the postal system

male: a man or boy

much: great in quantity

my: used by a speaker in referring to himself or herself

they'd: they had or they would

throne: the chair of state for a king

thrown: hurled

toe: one of the ending digits of the human foot

tow: to pull or haul by a vehicle

windmill: a machine driven by the force of the wind

witch: an ugly or mean old woman

wolf: a large wild mammal of the dog family

worse: not good

worst: very bad

yarn: thread made of fibers and used for knitting and weaving

yolk: the yellow of an egg

you've: you have

Answers

2. C, A, B	36. B, C, A	72. G, F, H
3. D, D	37. A, A	73. F, H
4. A, C, A	38. C, A, C	74. F, G, F
5. C, B	39. A, C	75. G, F
6. C, A, C	40. A, C, A	76. G, F, G
7. D, C	41. B, C	77. F, E
8. A, C, B	42. A, C, A	78. F, H, F
9. C, D	43. C, A	79. E, F
10. C, D, C	44. B, A, C	80. H, F, G
11. A, D	45. A, C	81. F, E
12. A, C, B	46. A, C, D	82. G, H, G
13. C, D	47. C, A	83. F, G
14. A, D, A	48. D, A, C	84. E, F, E
15. D, C	49. B, D	85. F, E
16. D, A, D	50. A, C, A	86. F, E, F
17. A, D	51. C, A	87. E, F
18. A, D, A	54. F, E, H	88. G, E, F
19. C, A	55. G, F	89. G, H
20. C, D, C	56. H, F, E	90. F, G, F
21. D, A	57. F, G	91. G, F
22. D, C, A	58. F, G, F	92. H, F, G
23. B, A	59. H, G	93. F, F
24. D, A, C	60. F, F, G	94. G, F, H
25. B, C	61. F, G	95. F, G
26. A, B, C	62. F, H, F	96. H, F, E
27. B, C	63. G, F	97. G, F
28. A, C, D	64. G, F, F	98. G, F, G
29. A, B	65. H, F	99. G, G
30. C, A, A	66. H, F, E	100. E, G, E
31. B, A	67. G, F	101. G, E
32. B, C, B	68. G, F, G	102. G, H, G
33. C, A	69. F, G	103. E, G
34. B, C, B	70. F, H, F	
35. A, A	71. H, F	